DORM ROOM FENG SHUI

DORM ROOM FENG SHUI

GINA MEYERS

Serenity Press Inc.

CONTENTS

DORM ROOM FENG SHUI
Compiled by
Gina Meyers

So you are getting ready to go off to college. Congratulations, this is an exciting time in your life. You desire it to be a smooth transition full of peace and harmony. You have your new mini refrigerator, your first checking account, a part-time job, a microwave, pencils, your ipad, a new wardrobe and a new college life. With *Dorm Room Feng Shui,* you get time tested advice on how to arrange your space. No matter how big or small, you can produce peace and harmony in your new environment. *Dorm Room Feng Shui* presents quick, inexpensive, and easy cures to enhance your environment. You will feel all the creature comforts of home and be organized as well. As an added bonus, the feng shui guide gives you quick fixes to cure your troubles and improve every area of life. You might want to put a small plant in the corner of your room, a sea shell or even a red envelope. When you've added elements to your environment that you find pleasing, you will enhance your life and make significant changes without a lot of effort or hassle. As an added bonus, there are dorm room friendly recipes for you to try, a how-to create a successful budget in college, a special section on how to make a dream board, simple mental exercises to keep you sharp, a handy journal to note your progress and chronicle your college life experience.

The Eight Keys to Balance

Life is a juggling act, finding the right formula for balance is essential. Below are the eight important categories of spiritual, emotional, career, family, financial, social, physical, and mental. Meditate and visualize each category and think of four things that you can do to improve in each area. Use this worksheet yearly to check your progress.

SPIRITUAL

1. _______________________________________
2. _______________________________________
3. _______________________________________
4. _______________________________________

EMOTIONAL

1. _______________________________________
2. _______________________________________
3. _______________________________________
4. _______________________________________

CAREER

1. _______________________________________
2. _______________________________________
3. _______________________________________
4. _______________________________________

FAMILY

1. __________________________________
2. __________________________________
3. __________________________________
4. __________________________________

FINANCIAL

1. __________________________________
2. __________________________________
3. __________________________________
4. __________________________________

SOCIAL

1. __________________________________
2. __________________________________
3. __________________________________
4. __________________________________

PHYSICAL

1. __________________________________
2. __________________________________
3. __________________________________
4. __________________________________

MENTAL

1. _______________________________
2. _______________________________
3. _______________________________
4. _______________________________

Five Elements To Produce Harmony In Your Environment

There are five key elements to creating balance in your environment and they are Fire, Earth, Metal, Water, and Wood. Each room in your home or office space needs the five elements. The Environment will feel comforting and serene when all of the five elements are represented in equal numbers. When your level of consciousness is raised concerning the importance of a room, you will "sense" if all of the elements are in balance or if some are missing.

1. FIRE
2. EARTH
3. METAL
4. WATER
5. WOOD

Fire is represented by the color Red. Fireplaces, sunlight, lighting, candles, leather, wood objects, triangles, and cone shapes all are representative of Fire. Earth is represented by the color yellow, ceramic objects, brick, tile, stucco, soil, square, and rectangular shapes. Metal is represented by the color white, rocks, stones, or metal objects, a circle or oval shapes. Water is created by the colors black, dark blue, or grey, with glass and crystals and mirror, and flowing asymmetrical shapes. Wood is represented by the color green, plants, flowers and things made of wood and pillar and column shapes.

Six Inexpensive Cures to Health, Wealth, and Prosperity

1. Candles
2. Mirrors
3. Cleaning
4. Plants
5. Clutter Free
6. Paint

Candles are a very inexpensive way to Feng Shui or arrange your environment. Pleasing scents bring an aroma of peace and calm, or love and excitement to your environment. Mirrors are excellent cures for money and safety issues. Place a mirror over your stove top as to not startle the cook while he or she is preparing food. Hanging a Mirror on the left wall from the doorway and placing nine coins or crisp dollar bills will assist in the accumulation of wealth. Having a clean house will give you the peace of mind to feel relaxed and happy in your home and environment, it will help rid your body of anxiety. Plants produce oxygen and we need oxygen as humans to breath. Bring nature indoors, if you suffer from allergies, plastic plants are preferable, just make sure to clean the leaves off with warm water and dishwasher detergent every few months so as to not accumulate dust in your home. A clutter free home means everything in its place and orderly. If you don't have a system, create one whereby you donate, throw away or put away. If stuffing something in the closet creates a clutter free environment, do it, just get it out of your sight. Painting is an excellent, inexpensive way to change the mood and look of a room.

Principle One

The first principle states that everything in the world, including your home and all of its contents, is alive and has vital energy that is called Ch'i. When you view the world in this way, belongings such as furniture, artwork, clothing, kitchenware, are transformed into living things that stimulate specific thoughts, memories, and feelings.

Wind Ch'i is considered the internal well-being in your life and water Ch'i is the outer world. Both environments affect one another, so it is essential that one's home environment has possessions that are positive and bring the owners good fortune.

Understanding the "Yin" and "Yang" Energy

The "Yin" and "Yang" are complimentary natural forces that are basic to all existing things. Everything in the universe can be placed into a category of either "Yin" or "Yang." The goal in life is the balance the energies of the elements of the "Yin" and "Yang" in the home as well as the office. The goal of the "Yin" and "Yang" is to is to be aware of the importance of maintaining balance in the face of change. The "Yin" and "Yang" represents and embodies the concept of "Perfect Balance", or harmony". Some people refer to the "Yin" and "Yang" as the "Path of life" or the "way or direction in life". By understanding the dynamic of the "Yin" and "Yang", you can become more aware and better equipped to quickly find balance in your environment.

Comparing and Contrasting "Yin" and "Yang" Qualities

Yin	Yang
Female	Male
Dark	Bright
Soft	Hard
Cold	Hot
Meek.	Aggressive
Rain	Sunshine
Round	Sharp
Mother	Father
Odd numbers	Even numbers
Winter	Summer
Moon	Sun

The Rules For Being Human

1. You will receive a body. You may love it or hate it, but it will be yours for the rest of your life. As you grow and mature, you may begin to see your body as a vehicle that carries you through life.
2. You will learn many lessons. Look at your life as being enrolled in full time school, life 101.
3. There are no mistakes or failures in life, only lessons. You will only grow when you have failures, but keep on trying. When successes happen, it will be exhilarating, however, you'll learn more from your mistakes than your successes.
4. There will be lessons that show up again and again. These lessons will be presented in different forms and repeated until you have learned. Then, once you have passed that particular class (or lesson), you will be able to go on to your next lesson.
5. Learning lessons is like life long learning. There is no end date; there are plenty of classes to take and plenty of lessons to learn. School is never out of session. Luckily, no tuition is required.
6. Life turns out the way your higher power deems fit. The cliché, the grass is greener on the other side of the fence is a fallacy. The life you have is the one you are meant to have based upon choices and plans you've made with your own free will. Everyone at one time or another thinks life should turn out differently. But, alas, there is the rub. Everyone thinks that, sometimes there is a better life, or a better situation, and sometimes there is, so in essence, we help to mold our destinies, but fail to see that it is never about us and we are never truly in control. Our higher power is at work 24 hours a day seven days a week.

7. Timing is everything, but it isn't our time to control, fix, mold, shape, destroy, or otherwise interfere with the higher powers plan.

8. The vertical relationship with the Higher Power is primary to our earthly happiness that opens our hearts and minds to the horizontal relationship with our earthly cohabitants.

9. The key to happiness lies within.

10. Your life lessons will come to you regardless of your plans or actions. Although no one gets to choose their classes at Life 101, you do get the choice to choose how you react to your life experiences. You can choose to be bitter or better. You will have all of the tools and resources that you need. What you make of your life is up to you, the choice of how to live it is up to you, but your Higher Power will be your personal tour guide on the journey.

11. The powerful life lessons are always at your disposal everyday. As you become more in tune with your intuition, feelings, gut instinct, you life will exist on a higher, more evolved state. This state is called awareness and being aware will help you to change and grow. The process will make some unexpected twists, turns, like a roller coaster ride. Sometimes you might even feel sick from the ride or think that something went wrong, but sometimes, when you reflect upon it and dig deep inside, you will be able to acknowledge that the "failures", "disasters" are part of your Higher Powers plan for your life.

12. Suddenly growth will happen, you will feel in touch with yourself and others around you and you no longer will look at things as Fear based, now everything will be Love Based.

<u>**Ideas for storage**</u>

Use a boogie board to serve as a cork board. Mini chalk board for messages.

There are so many cooking products on the market to make your time away at college beneficial. The list is for products that you could easily store after cooking in your dorm room closet or in your first apartment. These products will help with cooking in a small space and are designed for cooking for one or two people.

Budget

Income/salary from all sources	
Investment income	
Other income	
Savings	
Total Monthly Income	

Monthly Expenses
Home

Mortgage/rent/HOA	
Landscaping	
Laundry	

Gas	

Electricity	
Water	
Home Phone	
Cell phone	
Internet	
Misc.	

Total Monthly Income

-Total Monthly Expenses	
=Net Cash Flow	

Dream Board For Your Dorm Room

Creating Focused intentions through manifesting your dreams by visualizing and realizing what your dreams are.

How To Make a Dream board

Gather Materials:

You can either use magazines or images found on websites. If you choose to use magazines, gather different types of magazines, so you can cover all the topics that you are interested in. For instance, if you are interested in traveling, visiting a local travel agency and requesting brochures on the countries you would like to visit. If you are interested in Yoga for instance, purchasing a magazine devoted to Yoga, health and wellness would be appropriate. You can also use documents you collect or bulletins, found at your local church or university. You want to find images that remind you of your goals and ambitions, hopes, dreams for your future. These images are meant to motivate.

Cut out images:

Go through each magazine and cut out any pictures, inspirational words that appeal to you. Allow your mind to wander and follow your instinct. Find bright, colorful images that make you feel ambitious, motivated, exhilarated, fantastic. Ideas are: nice houses, cars, flowers, landmarks, fitness models, powerful words (love, hope).

Purchase a board or purchase a kit:

A large blank poster board, inexpensive and available at a local art store or dollar store, discount drug store/pharmacy. You can also invest in a canvas, cork or a magnet board.

Cut and paste pictures:

Cut and paste pictures on your dream board. You can use glue sticks, or non-toxic glue.

Place the dream board:

Put it beside your bed, or in your office, or in your workspace. If you don't have a lot of room, take a picture of your dream board and look at it on your phone or print out a photograph of your dream board. It will be a smaller version, so good for handy reference to keep in your glove box of your car.

Over the course of a year, you will notice that you will start to achieve some of your dreams that you have placed on your board.

Steps to Achieving all of your Dreams and Goals....

1. Get a clear vision of what you want to create. Hold that vision in your mind as often as possible every single day. See it in your mind, and feel it throughout your body as if it is happening right now. If you visualize it, your brain has the capacity to activate the feelings that come with that picture. This is what Olympic athletes do regularly when focusing on the "win".

2. Say "yes" to those opportunities and events that are in alignment with your dreams and take massive action every single day towards manifesting and achieving your goals and dreams.

3. Say "no" to anything that veers you away or steer you away from your true bliss, your true calling found in your brightest visions. Unless you make room for your new dreams, you will stay stuck with what you don't want rather than attracting and keeping what you do want.

4. Every 21st day of the month, make a plan for keeping your life in balance by making a "New Year's Resolution" once a month on the 21st. The plan helps for change on a monthly basis so you can adjust by making big or small changes monthly towards positive change in your life. It is a way to make goals and to see the fruits of your labor more efficiently. The main advantage of the plan is it helps keep your life in balance. So here is a plan that helps manage change while helping to maintain a balance in your

life at the same time. Here is how it works. Check in with yourself once a month and see if you are keeping your life in balance while meeting goals that you have set for yourself and then setting new goals as needed. It's, therefore, a time for personal reflection. Choosing the 21st of each month is because it is the shortest day of the year (Dec. 21st) and it is also the longest day of the year on the 21st (June 21st) and the seasons traditionally change on the 21st (Sept.—autumn), (Dec.—winter), (Mar.—spring), (June—summer) but any day of the month will do. The main point is to choose one day a month and have it be the same day each month. You can mark the day on your physical calendar, your online calendar, you can even set your cell phone alarm clock for the same day each month so you will not forget. Evaluate your life in nine areas and add goals that seem especially important, or just notes or random thoughts or an overall evaluation of your life. Here are the nine areas: Spiritual, Family, Love, Work, Physical, Mental/Education, Friendships, Financial, and Social.

A-Z Intention Exercise

Set your intention for in the morning:

"The only thing I need is to feel good." This is going to be a great day!

A-Z Feel-Good Exercise

Drink a green smoothie, juice, take your vitamins

(If you like tea, or coffee, or even espresso, you may)

The important thing about the morning is to be happy and to feel alive. Eating a balanced breakfast with at least a component of protein (in whatever form you prefer, toast with almond butter, an apple with peanut butter,

Morning Meditation

Stretching exercises

Walking

Prayer

Chanting

(Singing or dancing)

What are some things you can do in the morning to feel energized and alive?

Dream Categories

If you had no obstacles, what would you dream of doing? Would you run a marathon, learn to dance, meditate, speak in public, travel? Greatness begins by visualizing your dreams. Dreamers do and they achieve because of what they see and believe.

1) Love and Romance

Choose pictures that are a step or two beyond what you think you can attain, but are believable.

2) Wealth and Prosperity

Abundance

3)Career and Life Path

School, being a mom, being a dad, your profession are all part of your life path.

4)Health & Wellness

5)Mind & Soul

6)Synchronicity

7) Travel & Adventures

8) Reputation

Social life, how you want to make your mark, your impact

9) Creativity & Hobbies

10) Family

Why Dream?

We need to dream.

We have an incredible ability to heal ourselves and catch our dreams to improve our health.

Pay attention to capture your dreams through the tone of the emotion that you are feeling during the dream state. Waking day moments are filed and put away in our dreams, you can move on through your dreams to make your next waking day positive and happy.

Positive effects of Dreams:

Reduce our cortisol level

Helps us identify goals

Revelation of our life purpose

Dreams create invention, have to see it in your minds reality. Seeds of creation, collage all of your dreams,

Tips on How to Tap Into Our Life Purpose (tapping into your life purpose can be a great tool with Feng Shui).

There are so many things that can assist us in developing and honing in on our life purpose. Day dream, use your imagination, meditate, all of these things will help you to revel your life purpose. Dreams create invention, you have to dream it and see it to make it happen. You have to be able to see it in your minds reality, these are the seeds of creation, your dreams. Plant your garden of dreams, nuture it, water it, and you will see them grow. Make a collage of all of your dreams. Tapping into your life purpose involves planning and feeling. Think of your dreams as two magnets.

Two Magnets for your Dreams/Life Purpose

One magnet is on your heart, the other magnet is outside waiting to be activated. The Universe will match your magnetic vibration and the co-creators of the world will be magnetized towards helping you achieve your goals.

Quick tips:

Focus your intentions

Save magazine articles and photos that represent things you desire.

Keep it organized, utilize my easy steps for creating a Dream Board

Feel joy, in order to be focused on your dreams, feel joy in the moments.

Feeling joy activates our happy hormones.

Connect to things we are visualizing.

You must believe that you are worthy to manifest these dreams, this creates a stronger bond.

When you are aligned each day you manifest your dreams.

Get in your genius zone by being in alignment with your soul

Your Dream GPS

Easy steps to find your core values and your life purpose.

What are your core values? This will help you to easily locate these.

Write down three adjectives from your favorite book, movie, a cartoon, or your favorite character.

Then jot down three words that come to mind. These are your three words for the year for your core values and your life purpose.

Imagine Your Dream Destination:

Set a destination worthy of you.

Think BIGGER

Holistic Healing Exercises

Questions:

How has disease manifested in your physical body as a result of mental, emotional, or spiritual stress?

What is blocking your ability to give and receive love?

Ritual Chant:

"I am tho" mantra

Ra = sun energy

Ma = moon energy

Da = earth energy

Sa = infinity, universal energy

Sa = repeated

Say = the personal embodiment of Sa

So = the personal sense of merger with Sa

Hung = the Infinite, vibrating and real

Mundra Exercise:

Bend the arms and bring the elbows against the side of the rib cage. The palms of the hands face the sky. The elbows are snug at your sides with the forearms in close to your upper arms. The hands are at a 45 degree angle, halfway between pointing forward and pointing to the sides.

Healing Exercise:

Inhale deeply, hold your breath and visualize the person you want to send healing to. Make that image in your mind very clear and see a glowing green light around the person. Keeping that person in your mind, exhale. Inhale deeply, hold your breath and continue to send the person healing green light. Still keeping that vision in your mind, exhale. For the last time, inhale deeply, hold your breath and see the person very clearly, see the green healing light bathing the person, bathing every cell in the body. Exhale and relax.

Health Exercise:

Sitting cross-legged on the floor, inhale and take your shoulders up high towards your ears.

As you exhale drop your shoulders down and push your shoulder blades together, opening out your chest. Repeat a few times until the stiffness starts to leave your body. Breathe deeply to help shift the tightness.

Inhale and take the shoulders forward and drop the head down to create more space for the shoulders.

As you exhale, move your shoulders back in a circular motion. To repeat the exercise, inhale and take your shoulders forwards and up, then exhale taking them back and down. Keep all your movements fluid and graceful. Return to the start position. As you exercise, keep still, concentrating on your neck and shoulders.

Visualization Exercise:

Kneel with a straight back, relaxed jaw and softened face. Imagine the energy from the base chakra. Feel it move up through the spine up to the crown chakra at the top of the head to join with the cosmic energy. It is then that the principles of life become clear and the mind, body, and spiritual selves are unified. then that the principles of life become clear and the mind, body, and spiritual selves are unified.

Journaling
Why Journal?

What is journaling? Journaling is an act of free-thinking writing or "informal writing" as a regular practice with some goal in mind. Usually, journals serve as a creative outlet for the journalist. The purpose of journaling is different for different people, such as recording thoughts, practicing their writing craft, emotional healing through writing, or cataloging ideas as they occur to the writer/journaler. Oftentimes in life, we label experiences as "right" or "wrong". This black and white thinking becomes a problem after many years of habitual labeling. If we can simply change our vocabulary through the art of journaling or "writing", we can "right" the way we think about life and situations. In this book, you will be guided through time tested, thought provoking writing prompts and inspirational messages to tap into your total transformation. Use your journal to heal from chronic stressful ways of looking at life and transform yourself through learning your story. It's never been a better time to write your story.

Journal Tips to help get your started:

1. *Get creative*
2. *Use journal writing prompts*
3. *Find journaling techniques that work for you*
4. *Let go of judgements, write for you!*
5. *Let go of the need to write as if it is an English paper that will be graded.*
6. *Create a writing schedule*
7. *Create a writing routine*

MY College JOURNAL

MY   JOURNAL   IS   FOR   THE   PURPOSE   OF:

____

____

____

____

MY JOURNAL WILL BE USED TO HELP ME EXPRESS MYSELF AND BETTER UNDERSTAND THE EVENTS THAT HAVE IMPACTED ME SO THAT I WILL BE ABLE TO:

Success is what you attract by being attractive

How will Feng Shui Help You?

—

Cooking and Steaming:

1. Single Burner portable Buffet Range

(also comes in a Double burner Portable buffet Range)

The easy-to-use design is compact for lightweight portability with a variable temperature control knob so you can cook or keep food warm at just the right temperature. The single burner coil distributes heat evenly, while a handy power indicator light provides added peace of mind and ease during use.

- Lightweight for easy portability
- Cooking convenience
- Dual adjustable temperature control knobs
- Cook or keep warm
- Coil burner design distributes heat evenly for better results
- Power indicator light for burner provides peace of mind and extra security during use

1. 3-in-1 Grill-Griddle-Waffle Maker

Start off by making waffles, then reverse the cooking plates and fold back the hinged top it opens flat into 2 griddles plates for cooking eggs and bacon. Cooking healthy is easy with the grease channels that drain oily residues away from your foods. For lunch, make toasty sandwiches that will satisfy any appetite.

- Cook a Wide Assortment of Family Meals
- Opens Flat Into Two Griddle Plates
- Adjustable Temperature Knob

- Grease Run-Off Channels
- Power Indicator Light
- Cool-Touch Handles
- Reversible Nonstick Grill and Waffle plates

3) 3-Cup Rice Cooker

With the heavy-duty tempered glass lid, you can see the cooking process while the nonstick, removable cooking bowl makes cleanup a breeze. You can cook up healthy and warm rice quick and easy. Jasmine, Brown Rice, etc.

- Exceptional Performance
- Makes Great Tasting Rice, Automatically Keeps it Warm and Ready to Serve
- Ultimate Convenience
- Cook and Warm Indicator Lights
- Keep Warm Cycle
- Cool-Touch Handles
- Easy Cleaning
- Nonstick Cooking Bowl
- Tempered Glass Lid
- Serving Scoop
- Rice Measuring Cup

1. Single Serve Coffee Maker
2. 2 Slice Toaster

Other ideas for your dorm room.
Countertop Toaster Oven
2 in 1 food processor and blender
Cabbage Jalapeno Slaw
2 Whole Jalapenos
¼ cup of cherry tomatoes
½ cup of cilantro leaves

1 lime, fresh squeezed juice

2 Tablespoons of Olive Oil

2 Tablespoons of lemon juice

Salt and pepper to taste

1 whole cabbage, shredded

1/8 cup of shredded carrots

Directions: in a cuisnert, mix jalapenos, cilantro, carrots, cherry tomatoes. In a large bowl, place shredded cabbage, next, mix jalapeno mixture. Add olive oil, lemon juice, lime juice and salt and pepper and blend with a wooden spoon. Place in the refrigerator for ½ hour to chill.

Tomato Caprese Salad

4 large ripe tomatoes, sliced ¼ inch thick

1/3 cup fresh basil leaves, washed and dried (can substitute dried basil)

Salt and pepper to taste

1 pound of fresh mozzarella, sliced ¼ inch thick (can purchase mozzarella balls in snack size, easy to use if you are making a salad for one)

6 Tablespoons of Extra Virgin Olive Oil

3 Tablespoons of Balsamic

Directions: On a large platter, alternate and overlap tomato slices, mozzarella cheese slices, and basil leaves. Drizzle olive oil and balsamic vinegar and season with salt and pepper. May place in the fridge to chill for ½ hour and may eliminate vinegar and add more olive oil if desired.

Basil Pesto

1 cup of olive oil

1 head of garlic, cloves, peeled

2 cups of fresh basil leaves, divided

1 cup fresh flat leaf parsley, leaves, divided.

½ cup of pine nuts

½ teaspoon of salt.

1 cup of grated Parmesan cheese

¼ cup of grated Romano cheese

Directions: in a blender, combine half of the ingredients, basil, parsley, pine nuts, salt, garlic and oil. Pulse about 20 times, or until coarsely chopped. Scrape the sides of the food processor. Process for about an additional 2 minutes and add additional oil, if needed. At this point, you may pulse until a paste forms. Transfer to a mixing bowl and repeat the process with the other half of the ingredients, minus the cheeses. Once completed into a paste form, mix the cheeses in the mixing bowl with the paste. You may toast the pine nuts for a few minutes in a skillet over low heat. Another option would be to add a ¼ cup of shredded cheddar cheese and pecan or walnuts instead of pine nuts.

Grape and Orange Turkey Salad

1 cup of diced turkey breasts (purchased at the deli counter, ask for ½ inch thick slices of your favorite turkey, Lean Turkey Breast, Smoked Turkey, etc.) Also, they sell Turkey Breast already cooked in the meat aisle of the grocery store).

1/2 cup of red or green seedless grapes, halved

1/4 cup of thinly sliced celery (1 stalk of celery)

¼ cup of sliced almonds, toasted and coarsely chopped

1 Tablespoon of chopped red or yellow onion (may also use onion flakes)

1/8 cup of goat cheese

1 medium orange, peeled, sectioned and cut into bite-size pieces (or one can of Mandarin Oranges, purchase the can with the easy pull top off so you don't need to hassle with a can open)

1/2 bag of bagged lettuce such as Spring Mix, Spinach, or Garden Variety Salad

Salt and pepper

Dressing

Juice of ½ medium orange

½ teaspoon of Dijon mustard

½ teaspoon of salt

¼ teaspoon of ground black pepper

2 Tablespoons of olive oil

Directions: Can wash the lettuce in the bag and drain, use a paper towel or two to absorb excess water. Can also wash and clean the lettuce in a salad spinner. Make the dressing in a airtight plastic container seal and shake. Extra salad can stay in your dorm refrigerator for up to 48 hours.

Spinach, Apple, and Pecan Salad

2 Tablespoons of extra virgin olive oil

1 1/2 Tablespoons of cider. Vinegar

1 Tablespoon of prepared mustard

1 Tablespoon of sugar

1/2 teaspoon of Salt

1/4 teaspoon of pepper

Green or red apples, cut into bite sized pieces

1/4 cup of thinly sliced red onion

Bag of washed fresh spinach leaves

1/2 cup toasted pecans

Directions: In a large bowl, whisk together the oil, vinegar, mustard, sugar, salt, and pepper. Just before serving, add apples, onions, spinach, and pecans. Toss until well coated with dressing.

Fig and Arugula Salad with Parmesan

2 Tablespoons of minced shallots

1 ½ Tablespoons of balsamic vinegar

1 Tablespoon of olive oil

¼ teaspoon of salt

16 fresh figs, each cut in half lengthwise

6 cups of trimmed arugula

¼ teaspoon of freshly ground cracked black pepper

¼ cup of shaved fresh Parmesan cheese

Directions: Combine the first four ingredients in a large bowl, beat with a whisk. Next, add figs and let marinate in the juices for twenty minutes. Add the arugula and pepper, top with Parmesan cheese. Serves four.

Simple Salad

Butter lettuce

Sliced strawberries

Sliced grapes

Sliced apples

4 ounces of vanilla or lemon yogurt

Honey roasted peanuts

1 Tablespoon of honey

2 Tablespoon vinegar

1 Tablespoon olive oil

Salt and pepper to taste

Directions: Mix the ingredients together. Place lettuce on a plate and decorate with the fruit and sprinkle with honey roasted nuts.

Broccoli Raisin Salad

1 purple onion, thinly sliced

1 package of fresh broccoli florets

1 cup golden raisins

1 cup mayonnaise

4 bacon slices, cooked and crumbled

2 Tablespoons red wine vinegar

Directions: In a salad bowl, toss ingredients together, then chill in the refrigerator for at least two hours.

Cobb Salad

A medium head of lettuce, shredded (Ice Berg)

3 hard boiled eggs, cooked and diced (can purchase eggs already cooked, shelled)

8 or so slices of Bacon, cooked and crumbled (can microwave bacon)

2 ½ cups of Chicken, cooked and cubed

1 large finely chopped Tomato, (Garden, Roma, Campari Variety)

1 large Avocado, pitted and cut up

4 sliced green onions

*Optional 3 ounces of shredded Cheddar Cheese (can purchase cheese already grated)

Dressing

1/3 cup Vinegar

1 teaspoon salt

¼ teaspoon pepper

½ teaspoon dry mustard

½ teaspoon sugar

1/8 teaspoon garlic powder

2/3 cup of vegetable oil

¼ cup of blue cheese crumbled

Directions: Wash and shred the lettuce. Place the shredded lettuce in a bowl. Arrange bacon, chicken, tomatoes, avocados in sections, with egg in the middle. May add shredded cheddar cheese and pour dressing over the Cobb Salad.

Spring Mix Salad with Strawberries, Walnuts and Goat Cheese

1 pint of fresh strawberries, rinsed, dried and stems cut off

5 ounces of Spring Mix

½ cup of walnut pieces, toasted

½ cup of crumbled goat cheese

Walnut Balsamic Vinaigrette

2 Tablespoons of balsamic vinegar

½ teaspoon of Dijon mustard

5 Tablespoons of Extra-Virgin Olive Oil

Salt and freshly ground black pepper

Directions: To prepare the vinaigrette, combine vinegar, mustard and both oils in a glass jar and seal the lid tightly. Shake the jar vigorously to combine. Season the vinaigrette with salt and pepper to taste. Vinaigrette can be refrigerated, covered, up to one month. Return to room temperature and shake vigorously before using.

Cut strawberries into quarters, place in a small bowl and toss with about 2 Tablespoons of the vinaigrette. Set aside. Place all of the spring mix in a large bowl and add 3 Tablespoons of the vinaigrette. Toss to lightly coat the leaves; then taste and add more vinaigrette if needed. Transfer the lettuce to individual salad plates. Top the lettuce with the strawberries, toasted walnuts and crumbled goat cheese. Serve immediately. You can use vinaigrette for a spinach salad too.

Cold Pasta Salad with Broccoli and Artichokes

1 pound bow tie pasta

1 bunch of Broccoli, halved

8-10 Pepperoni, cut into 1-inch strips

1 jar, (6.5 ounces) Marinated artichoke hearts, diced

1/2 cup sun-dried tomatoes

3 green onions, chopped

1 tablespoon red wine vinegar

1/4 teaspoon salt

1/4 teaspoon pepper

1/4 cup parmesan cheese

Directions: Cook pasta in lightly salted water for 10 minutes or until almost tender. Add broccoli to boiling water during the last 5 minutes of cooking and then drain. Add the cooked pasta and broccoli to a bowl along with the other ingredients, and toss. Serve hot or cold. Parmesan cheese as a topping, is optional.

The Well stocked Dorm Room Pantry

If you are going to entertain from your dorm room, or even just make yourself the occasional snack or meal (something more than a cup of soup) you will want to have these things on hand in your dorm room. Most of these items are small and can be stored together in a covered tote, like Rubbermaid. Even the food/seasonings can be put into a small covered tote to keep fresh and keep out ants.

Tools		Foods

Set of mixing bowls
Hot plate or electric
skillet, coffee pot,
multi-pot
Paring Knife
Chef's Knife
Cutting Board
Measuring cups and
spoons (liquid and dry)
Strainer
4 Quart pot
Small frying pan
(non-stick)
Rubber spatula
Wooden spoon
Re-sealable plastic food
containers
Small microwave safe
coffee / soup mug
Small microwave safe
cereal bowl and plates
2-4 spoon, soup spoon,
fork, and dinner knife

Salt
Pepper
Onion powder
Garlic powder
Cayenne pepper
Small bottle of olive oil
Small bottle of red
wine vinegar
Peanut butter
Honey
Cereal
Cookies
Trail mix
Crackers
Cereal bars
Juice boxes
Bottled water
Canned soup
Peanut butter
Instant oatmeal
Pasta
Instant coffee, cocoa,
tea
Microwaveable cups of
soup
Ramon instant soup &
noodles
Microwaveable
macaroni & cheese

No time for a Supermarket Run
<u>Substitutions</u>

If you are out of…..	Substitute
	1 teaspoon of baking soda and 2 teaspoons of cream of tartar
1 Tablespoon of baking powder	2 Tablespoons of flour
1 Tablespoon of cornstarch	½ cup evaporated milk mixed with ½ cup water
1 cup of milk	1 cup regular milk at room temperature plus 1 TBSP vinegar or lemon juice
1 cup buttermilk	
1 cup sugar	1 cup of honey, then reduce other liquid ingredients in recipe by ¼ cup

<u>Weights and Measures</u>

WeightSame as this Measure

1 pound of brown sugar 2 ½ cups of packed brown sugar

1 cup of granulated sugar 1 1/3 cups of granulated sugar

1 pound of powdered sugar 3 ½ cups of powdered sugar

1 pound of all purpose flour 4 cups of flour

12 egg yolks 1 cup of egg yolks

8-10 egg whites 1 cup of egg whites

3 teaspoons (tsp) 1 Tablespoon (TBSP)

2 Tablespoons 1/8 cup, or 1 ounce

4 Tablespoons ¼ cup, 2 ounces

5 1/3 Tablespoons 1/3 cup

8 Tablespoons ½ cup

10 2/3 Tablespoons 2/3 cup

12 Tablespoons ¾ cup

14 Tablespoons 7/8 of a cup

16 Tablespoons 1 cup or ½ pint, 8 ounces

2 cups1 pint

2 pints1quart

2 cups16 ounces

A dash equals slightly less than 1/8 of a teaspoon

Ounces/CupsMetric Equivalents

½ fluid ounce15 milliliters

2 fluid ounces60 milliliters

8 fluid ounces240 milliliters

16 fluid ounces480 milliliters

1/8 cup30 grams

¼ cup60 grams

1 cup240 grams

1 pound480 grams

<u>Cooking terms and Abbreviations</u>

Term/abbreviationDefinition

TBSP Tablespoon

tsp Teaspoon

ozOunces

lbPound

SautéCooking ingredients in a shallow pan with small amount of fat over relatively high heat

Preheat ovenTurn oven on to pre-determined temperature so that ingredients go into a hot oven, allowing for quicker, more even cooking.

Boil Bringing liquids to a boil means that the liquid has large bubbles breaking rapidly at the surface throughout the pan, not just small bubbles on the bottom or sides of pan.

Simmer To simmer foods, bring the liquid to a rapid boil then adjust temperature down to maintain a gentle boil.

Mince Very finely chopping an ingredient. The fine chopping allows more of the oils that provide flavor to be activated when added to recipes.

Dice Cut the ingredient into little cubes about the size of dice.

BrownCook meat or other ingredients in small amount of fat until a golden brown color is reached –does not mean to cook completely.

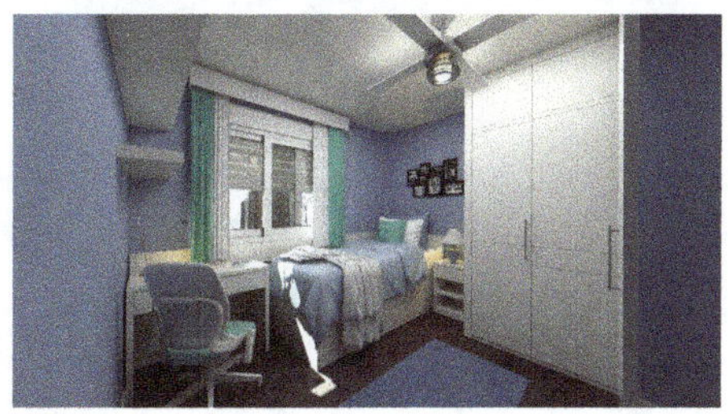